M000288269

This book is presented to

_____

on the occasion of

_____

by

_____

_____

Date

Dear Daddy

Dennis Rach

SAINT LOUIS

Scripture quotations taken from the HOLY BIBLE, NEW INTERNATIONAL VERSION®. NIV®. Copyright © 1973, 1978, 1984 by International Bible Society. Used by permission of Zondervan Publishing House. All rights reserved.

Copyright © 1999 Concordia Publishing House
3558 S. Jefferson Avenue, St. Louis, MO 63118-3968
Manufactured in the United States of America

All rights reserved. No part of this publication may be reproduced, stored in a retrieval system, or transmitted, in any form or by any means, electronic, mechanical, photocopying, recording, or otherwise, without the prior written permission of Concordia Publishing House.

1 2 3 4 5 6 7 8 9 10   08   07   06   05   04   03   02   01   00   99

Contents

Preface

*I*t's not easy being a husband, and it's especially hard being a daddy. I believe that, at heart, most men want to be good daddies and husbands, but it's hard to know how sometimes.

From personal experience, I know we all need occasional nudges (and sometimes a kick in the backside). We all need to be reminded that one of our greatest blessings from God comes in the form of our family. And one of our greatest gifts to God is having the kind of relationship with our family that our heavenly Father has with us. We can share His love with our wives, our children, and those around us by being the daddies He called us to be.

I must confess: If Jonathan and JuliAnne had really written the letters in this book, I would probably be in big trouble. I know I have a lot of learning and growing to do as a daddy and as a husband. So I write this book not as one who has achieved any sense of perfection, but as one who loves his Lord, his wife, and his kids. It is my prayer that these letters will help me and other men become the daddies God intended us to be.

This book is written to the glory of God. I can't thank Him enough for all the ways He has blessed me. I thank God for my daddy and his daddy, for Jon G., Harvey H., and the many other men who had a profound influence in shaping me into the father and husband I am today.

I am most thankful for the people who call me husband and daddy. Nikki is not only my wife but my best friend, ministry partner, supporter, and encourager. Jonathan and JuliAnne are very special gifts, and they have brought insurmountable joy to my life.

I love being a daddy. Thank You, God, for giving me this honor!

Husband

*Husbands, love your wives,
just as Christ loved the church
and gave Himself up for her.*

Ephesians 5:25

*Being a good daddy starts with
being a good husband.*

Dear Daddy,

   I saw you sneak up on Mommy and give her a big hug. She looked really surprised!

Love, Jonathan

Dear Daddy,

   It's really nice of you to open Mommy's car door for her, even when she doesn't have her hands full.

Love, Jonathan

Dear Daddy,

   You may not remember this in the morning, because your eyes are barely open, but thank you for comforting me at 4:00 A.M. so Mommy could sleep.

Love, JuliAnne

Dear Daddy,

    You must have a special calendar book. You mailed Mommy a card for the 10th year and 7th month anniversary of your first date!

Love, JuliAnne

Dear Daddy,

    It's fun to watch you play "kissy-monster" with Mommy like you do with me and JuliAnne.

Love, Jonathan

Dear Daddy,

    I heard Mommy tell you on the phone that we were pretty "trying" today. It was really nice of you to come home and give her a break by cooking supper. Next time, you just might want to order out.

Love, Jonathan

Dear Daddy,

   It was nice of you to bring Mommy flowers today. Did you pick them from our neighbor's rose garden? I hope not. She looks kind of cranky today!

Love, JuliAnne

Dear Daddy,

   I can tell you and Mommy team up when it comes to the rules in the house. Isn't that against the law? I can't get away with anything!

Love, Jonathan

Dear Daddy,

   I know you love Mommy because you say it and you show it. When I grow up, I will treat my wife the same way.

Love, Jonathan

Dear Daddy,

   The ways you say and show your love for Mommy make me feel safe and loved. I want to marry someone who will care for me the same way you care for Mommy.

Love, JuliAnne

10 Hints from Daddy

1. Tell your wife you love her five times each day.
2. Find seven ways each day to *show* your wife you love her.
3. Make time to be alone with your wife each day.
4. Ask your wife what her needs are as a wife and mommy. Do what you can to help meet those needs.
5. Ask your wife to give you some pointers on how you can be a better husband. Talk them through with your wife and work on them together.
6. Keep your wife on her toes—do something for her that you wouldn't normally do.
7. Make it possible for your wife to do something either alone or with her friends. Give her time away from the kids.
8. Treat your wife the same in private as you do in public: great!
9. Pray for both your wife and your marriage continually.
10. Remember, the daily investments you make in your marriage will reap years of interest.

Faith Development

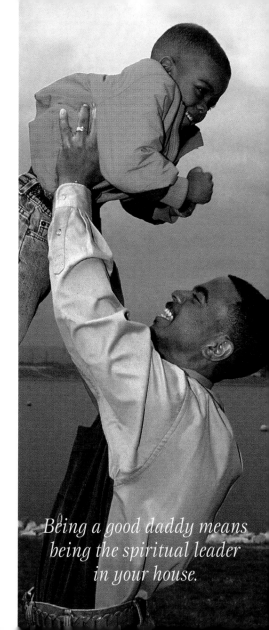

*L*ove the LORD your God
with all your heart and
with all your soul and
with all your strength.
These commandments
that I give you today
are to be upon your hearts.
Impress them on your children.
Talk about them
when you sit at home and
when you walk along the road,
when you lie down and
when you get up.

Deuteronomy 6:5–7

Being a good daddy means
being the spiritual leader
in your house.

Dear Daddy,

Thank you for picking godparents who love Jesus and who want to spend time sharing stories about Jesus with me.

Love, Jonathan

Dear Daddy,

Thank you for taking me to church. I can't wait to sing the songs with you. My favorite is "A Mighty Toy-Chest Is Our God." Amen!

Love, Jonathan

Dear Daddy,

I saw you reading your Bible today. How can you tell what it says? Your Bible doesn't have nearly as many pictures as mine does.

Love, JuliAnne

Dear Daddy,

I love to hear you tell the story about how Jesus let the little children come and be with Him even when the disciples said He was too busy. I know Jesus loves me and thinks I'm special.

Love, Jonathan

Dear Daddy,

Thank you for saying the words slowly when we say a blessing over our food. I like to pray with you and to thank God for giving us the food we need. (It also makes me feel like the food is safe to eat when you're the cook!)

Love, Jonathan

Dear Daddy,

Jesus loves me this I know, for my daddy tells me so.

Love, JuliAnne

Dear Daddy,

I really like it when you sing praise songs to me at bedtime. Maybe the money Grandma paid for your voice lessons wasn't a waste after all!

Love, Jonathan

Dear Daddy,

I know you can't always be around for me. Sometimes you have other places you have to be. Thank you for telling me Jesus will be with me always. That makes me feel good.

Love, JuliAnne

Dear Daddy,

I think it's pretty neat that when I ask to hold your hand and I say, "Pray," you do!

Love, Jonathan

Dear Daddy,

*I can tell you love Jesus by the things you say and
the way you act. I can tell Jesus is very important to you.*

Dear Daddy,

I have a secret to tell you: When you are rocking me at night and you think I'm asleep, sometimes I'm not. I hear you saying a special prayer for me. Thank you for loving me that way.

Love, Jonathan

10 Hints from Daddy

1. Faith is caught by your children. What bait are you using?
2. Tell your children five times each day that Jesus loves them.
3. Pray aloud whenever the opportunity arises.
4. Pick godparents not for sentimental reasons or family obligation but because they will assist you in raising your children in the Christian faith.
5. Sing a lot of praise songs with your children. Children love songs and are more apt to remember the songs you sing than the words you say.
6. Let your children worship with you as much as possible, even if they have the wiggles when they are little. Good habits start early.
7. Model personal faith growth by attending Bible class or Sunday school either with or at the same time as your children. Talk openly with them about what you learned in class and ask what they learned.
8. Have your child's godparents or some other significant adult hold you accountable as the spiritual leader in your house. Set goals and have the individual work with you to complete them.
9. Find an older male in your congregation whom you respect for the way he raised his children in the faith. Ask if he will serve as a mentor for you.
10. Pray ceaselessly for your children. Jesus Christ is the best gift you can give them.

Self-Esteem

*$\mathcal{A}$nd let us consider
how we may spur
one another on toward
love and good deeds.*

Hebrews 10:24

*Being a good daddy means
helping your children
feel good about who they are
as God's children.*

Dear Daddy,

Did you see me smile when you told Pastor how happy I make you? It makes me feel great to know that I make "happy Daddy."

Love, Jonathan

Dear Daddy,

I love to hear you say how beautiful I am to you, even when I'm having a bad hair day. (Of course, my bad hair days are nothing compared to your bad hairless days!)

Love, JuliAnne

Dear Daddy,

Can I always be your favorite firstborn son, even though JuliAnne was born this month?

Love, Jonathan

Dear Daddy,

It makes me feel good all over when you tell me you are proud of me.

Love, Jonathan

Dear Daddy,

How many pictures of us do you have in your office? It looks like a bizillion! Are you afraid you'll forget what we look like?

Love, JuliAnne

Dear Daddy,

You clap and cheer wildly when I pick up my toys. You even say, "Yeah, Jonathan!" It's kind of embarrassing when you do that—please don't stop.

Love, Jonathan

Dear Daddy,

You sure take a lot of pictures of me. I feel like a movie star!

Love, JuliAnne

Dear Daddy,

You think I'm ignoring you when I don't respond to your "I love you's," then you say it again. I don't answer because I know you'll keep on saying it and I like that.

Love, JuliAnne

Dear Daddy,

Thank you for letting me help put the clothes in the washing machine. I like to help!

Love, Jonathan

Dear Daddy,

When I hear you say, "You're Daddy's little girl," big smiles start in my heart and burst out of my face.

Love, JuliAnne

Dear Daddy,

I'm a big boy now and I want to do things for myself. Thanks for letting me try and for helping me when I figure out I still need your help on some things.

Love, Jonathan

Dear Daddy,
  Thank you for telling me
I am valuable because
I'm God's child.

                Love, JuliAnne

10 Hints from Daddy

1. Check your own self-esteem. It's easier for you to help your children develop a healthy self-esteem if yours is healthy too.

2. Model a positive attitude and outlook.

3. Help your children accomplish reasonable age-appropriate tasks and praise them when they do.

4. Don't take yourself too seriously. Don't be afraid to laugh at yourself when you mess up.

5. Praise your children but not generically. Point out specific things they do well.

6. Give your children the freedom to try new things. Encourage them without being pushy or making them feel uncomfortable.

7. Teach your children that seeking help is not a sign of weakness.

8. Help your children to value the contributions of others.

9. Teach your children to respect themselves.

10. Love your children, but show them you like them too.

Values

$\mathcal{T}$rain a child
in the way he should go,
and when he is old
he will not turn from it.

Proverbs 22:6

*Being a good daddy
means imparting wisdom
about what is really
important in life.*

Dear Daddy,

Thank you for letting me have some money to put into the offering plate at church. (Although I really think you ought to give me more to put in.)

Love, Jonathan

Dear Daddy,

Thank you for coming right away when I call. It makes me feel really important to you.

Love, JuliAnne

Dear Daddy,

Can I please have the keys to the car? (Did you notice I used proper manners? That should be good for something.)

Love, Jonathan

Dear Daddy,

Why do you get so excited when I say please and thank you?

Love, Jonathan

Dear Daddy,

When I say I'm sorry, thank you for forgiving me and giving me lots of hugs.

Love, JuliAnne

Dear Daddy,

This morning before you left for work, you promised we would play when you got home. I waited all day long for you to come home. Thank you for remembering and keeping your promise to me.

Love, Jonathan

Dear Daddy,

I like that there are lots of hugs around here.

Love, JuliAnne

Dear Daddy,

After we bought our slurpees, you let me put some money in the donations jar. Thanks for letting me help other people.

Love, Jonathan

Dear Daddy,

    That was nice of you to help the lady change her tire. Why did we turn down her offer of $10? We could've bought a lot of slurpees with that. Does "servanthood" mean never taking money for helping people?

Love, Jonathan

Dear Daddy,

    I'm glad you're more worried about how our family gets along than how much money you make. (Just a reminder though—my senior prom is coming up in 17 years. You'd better start saving!)

Love, JuliAnne

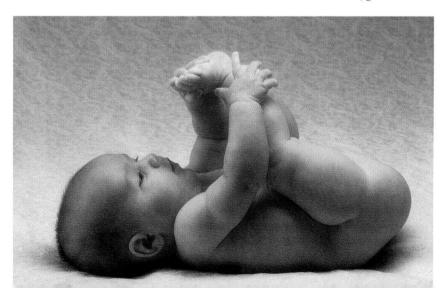

Dear Daddy,
   I'm glad you didn't
work late tonight.
I like to see you before
I go to bed.
            Love, JuliAnne

10 Hints from Daddy

1. Pray for wisdom that the values you currently hold are values that are pleasing to God.

2. Talk openly with your child about your values, especially if he questions something.

3. Remember, there is more to happiness than the amount of your paycheck.

4. Share your faith in God with your children.

5. Help your child to see herself as a valuable child of God.

6. Seek excellence in all you do. Teach your children that excellence is a worthy goal, not an unexpected accident.

7. Teach your children to love life.

8. Guide your children in respecting all God has created.

9. Help your children think through possible outcomes and to make choices on their own.

10. Understand that your "job" is to share with your children what is important to you and why. Don't force your values on them. They will claim for themselves what is important to them.

Training

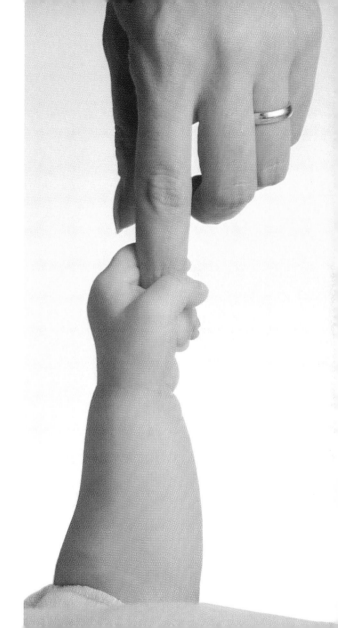

*F*athers, do not
exasperate your
  children; instead,
bring them up
  in the training
    and instruction
      of the Lord.

Ephesians 6:4

*Being a good daddy means
helping children
learn right from wrong.*

Dear Daddy,

*You said bedtime is 7:00 P.M. I said it is 10:00 P.M.
I'm glad you saw things my way and let me stay up
until 7:30.*

Love, JuliAnne

Dear Daddy,

*I like it when you give me choices. Maybe next time,
I can be the one who tells me what the choices are, OK?*

Love, Jonathan

Dear Daddy,

*Mommy says you have things backwards. I'm the
one who is supposed to go into time out when I throw a
temper tantrum, not you.*

Love, JuliAnne

Dear Daddy,
    Thanks for
telling me when
I do things right
instead of always
telling me when
I do things wrong.
    Love, Jonathan

Dear Daddy,

If Jesus said to forgive 70 × 7, why am I in time out?

Love, JuliAnne

Dear Daddy,

Why does part of me feel glad you set rules for me and another part of me want to see how far over the lines I can go without being caught?

Love, Jonathan

Dear Daddy,

Aunt Sharon said she would teach me how to wrap you around my finger. Unfortunately, flashing my baby blues at you doesn't seem to be working right now. Can we postpone my punishment until after I get my eyes checked?

Love, JuliAnne

Dear Daddy,

If Jesus was willing to die on the cross to take away my sins, do you think He might be willing to do my time out for me too?

Love, JuliAnne

Dear Daddy,

    I painted the wall to "help you," but you had fire in your eyes when you left the room. When you came back a few minutes later, you hugged me and took pictures of me beside my painting. So, am I in trouble or what?

Love, Jonathan

Dear Daddy,

    Grandma said that when you were growing up, you swore you would never have rules and punishments for your children. How come you changed your mind?

Love, JuliAnne

10 Hints from Daddy

1. When disciplining a child, make sure the child knows he is still loved and it is his action you are unhappy with.
2. Remember that the root word of discipline is *disciple*. Sometimes punishment comes with discipling, but the end result should be helping the child to learn and grow.
3. Be consistent in applying the rules. Children get confused when they do something one minute that's OK, but they get in trouble for doing the same thing later on.
4. Decide with your wife what the rules and consequences will be. If you are united, the consistency will help your child uphold the rules. A child will be confused if a rule is enforced by one parent and not by the other.
5. Explain to your child the importance of a rule. Knowing why a rule is in place will help her want to keep it. It will also help her better understand the consequences if she breaks the rule.
6. If your child makes you incredibly mad, step away from the situation before dealing with him. Give yourself (and perhaps him too) a time out so you can respond in his best interest, not out of your own anger.
7. Know which battles are worth fighting.
8. Set routines—they help avoid potential rule violations.
9. Praise your children as often as possible when you "catch" them doing something right. They will be more inclined to do the right thing than to seek attention by breaking the rules.
10. Be fair and firm when dealing with your children. Let love be your guide in all matters.

Family Rituals

So then, just as you received
Christ Jesus as Lord,
continue to live in Him,
rooted and built up in Him,
strengthened in the faith
as you were taught,
and overflowing with thankfulness.

Colossians 2:6–7

Being a good daddy means helping
the children develop roots in a family where
they know they belong and are loved always.

Dear Daddy,

I like it when we have "boys' night out" every Monday night. We really tear up that indoor playground at McDonald's, don't we?

Love, Jonathan

Dear Daddy,

Thank you for the cake and for lighting my baptismal candle on the anniversary of my Baptism. It must be a special day to remember.

Love, JuliAnne

Dear Daddy,

I like it when we stop for slurpees on the way home from church on Wednesday nights. One thing, though, next time don't tell Mommy I'm drinking her slurpee. She always drinks mine then.

Love, Jonathan

Dear Daddy,

 It's fun when we all go driving at Christmastime, looking at people's lights and displays. Who do you think will win our "I'd hate to have their electric bill" award this year?

            Love, JuliAnne

Dear Daddy,

 It sure is fun when we go to the mall to get a hot dog at the food court, and then ride the indoor train. You don't have to ride the train with me, but I let you because I know that you like trains too.

            Love, Jonathan

Dear Daddy,

 I like the red plate we use to honor family members on special days. I think I should have at least one special day each week because I'm such a special girl, don't you think?

            Love, JuliAnne

Dear Daddy,
 I love going
to the beach
every July.
I love to build
sand castles and
take walks
on the beach.
Next time you
fall asleep,
I'm going to bury
you in the sand.
 Love, Jonathan

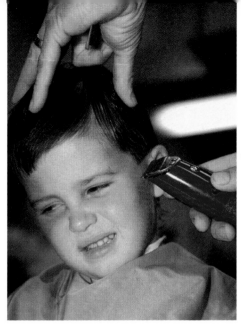

Dear Daddy,

It was fun to sneak up to that house and drop off some Christmas presents for the children. I'm just glad Mommy didn't honk the horn like last year.

Love, Jonathan

Dear Daddy,

I like it when we all say night-prayers together after bath time.

Love, JuliAnne

Dear Daddy,

It's a lot of fun when we all take a walk around the block. Please remember that I work twice as hard to keep up with you, so walk slowly or get on your knees, please.

Love, Jonathan

Dear Daddy,

I think we need a new family ritual. It's called "Take JuliAnne Shopping." I think Mommy should lead us. It would be so much fun. We could spend money and listen to Daddy groan. What do you think?

Love, JuliAnne

10 Hints from Daddy

1. The ultimate in family rituals is found in what the family does together to enhance spiritual growth among its members.
2. Developing family rituals helps provide a source of encouragement and support, especially as the children get older.
3. Remember that part of who your children are is developed by what you do together as a family.
4. Creating family rituals gives children a "belonging place" and helps them develop self-esteem.
5. Family rituals don't have to be long, drawn-out events. A regular time for the family to get ice cream together counts as a ritual.
6. The time you spend together in family rituals will open doors in your children's teen years so they know they have a safe place where they can be themselves and discuss personal issues.
7. As the children grow older and outgrow some of your rituals, allow them to help develop new rituals.
8. Make it a family ritual to work on a project together that will better someone else's family life. Carry it out anonymously.
9. Make sure that your rituals serve the needs of your family, not the other way around.
10. Make sure that family rituals include laughter—and lots of it!

Play

*There is a time for everything and
a season for every activity under heaven:
...a time to weep and a time to laugh,
a time to mourn and a time to dance.*

Ecclesiastes 3:1, 4

Being a good daddy means taking time to play.

Dear Daddy,

I love it when you make faces at me. You should see how silly you are. The people in the other car sure did.

Love, JuliAnne

Dear Daddy,

Thank you for turning off the football game to spend time with me. If you want, you can chase me with the ball and tackle me.

Love, Jonathan

Dear Daddy,

Mommy says that having kids around is just an excuse for you to act like a little boy again. I'm glad. I'll share my toys with you any time.

Love, JuliAnne

Dear Daddy,

I like to sit beside you on the couch, share pretzels, and watch the train video. It's my favorite movie. Are you sure you don't mind that it's the fourth time today we've watched it?

Love, Jonathan

Dear Daddy,

You've worked late three nights in a row now. Thanks for calling in "well" today and spending the day playing with me!

Love, JuliAnne

Dear Daddy,

I feel pretty cool when you push me on my three-wheeler. You need new batteries, though, because you run out of energy too quickly!

Love, Jonathan

Dear Daddy,

It's fun when you zoom me around the room like an airplane. Our crash landing was funny, so I don't know why you were crying. Next time, just be very careful not to trip over the dog.

Love, JuliAnne

Dear Daddy,

Can I sit on your lap and play the piano again? I promise I'm getting better. You won't even have to use the earplugs this time.

Love, Jonathan

Dear Daddy,

It's fun to play chase in the tubes at McDonald's playground. I'm sorry you got stuck, but I'm glad you got out before they called the fire department.

Love, Jonathan

Dear Daddy,

I saw you and Mommy tickling each other. You were laughing like two silly-birds and then you kissed. YUCK! That's gross—don't do that anymore!

Love, JuliAnne

Dear Daddy,

   I like to dance with you and I didn't mean to throw up on you. I just don't think I'm ready for the tango yet.

   Love, JuliAnne

10 Hints from Daddy

1. It's healthy for you to take time to relax and play.
2. It's even healthier for your family, especially your children, when you take time to relax and play.
3. Playing with your children lets them see an example of a well-rounded person, one who's not all work.
4. Playing with your children helps them learn appropriate times for playing and appropriate times for not playing.
5. Having playtime with your family creates a special closeness that can help you through times of difficulty or stress.
6. Playtime helps to provide balance and can often reduce stress from the outside that can affect your family.
7. Much can be taught about values and morals through playtime.
8. It's true that no daddy really wishes he had spent more time in the office, but every daddy wishes he had spent more time with his children.
9. When people share memories of a loved one, they usually share stories about fun times they had together. Give your children plenty to talk about.
10. Taking time to play sends a resounding "I love you" to your family.